Knitgrrl SOCKS & MITTS

Knitgrrl Socks & Mitts

ISBN 13 (print): 978-1-937513-92-4

First edition

Published by http://www.cooperativepress.com

Patterns, charts ©2019 Shannon Okey

Photos ©2019 Shannon Okey except pages 14, 17, 32, 36 (Amber Patrick)

Models: Arabella Proffer, Simone Renee Dugay, Nikol Lohr, Shannon Okey, Candra Squire and Shannon's trusty sock form

Cover wristwatch by The ExCB (theexcb.com) and bracelet by Bunny Paige (bunnypaige.com)

Every effort has been made to ensure that all the information in this book is accurate at the time of publication; however, Cooperative Press neither endorses nor guarantees the content of external links referenced in this book.

If you have questions or comments about this book, or need information about licensing, custom editions, special sales, or academic/corporate purchases, please contact Cooperative Press: info@cooperativepress.com or 10252 Berea Rd, Cleveland, Ohio 44102 USA

No part of this book may be reproduced in any form, except brief excerpts for the purpose of review, without prior written permission of the publisher. Thank you for respecting our copyright.

For Cooperative Press

Senior Editor: Shannon Okey

Technical Editor: Andi Smith

Knitgrrl SOCKS & MITTS

Cooperative Press
Cleveland, Ohio

Patterns

Gráinne, 6

Hildur, 10

Malus Mitts, 14

Milkmaid Mitts, 18

Rusla, 22

Schatzi, 28

Shiso, 32

Sweet Crocodile, 36

Valencia Marie, 40

Intro

This project was overambitious from the very beginning. I looked at my (considerable) yarn stash and declared a problem with the sheer amount. So naturally, I called my tech editor Andi Smith with a ridiculous idea: why not release a pattern a week for a year, and run a Patreon to help fund it? Yarn we had, but sample knitting is not cheap (nor should it be), and we also knew what other kinds of expenses to expect along the way after working on so many other projects together.

Andi is more than just my friend and tech editor. She is my co-conspirator, collaborator, enabler, right hand, left brain, and heart. We are teaching road trip road warriors, fiber show booth buddies, sounding boards, middle of the night text messagers and more. Without Andi's skills, this project would never have happened. She takes my gigantic, wild ideas and figures out how to make them reality, and she encourages me along the way without actually making me feel as if perhaps I should tone it down a bit. This book is part of the result!

You can find all the single patterns from this project on Ravelry:

> https://www.ravelry.com/patterns/sources/knitgrrl-patreon

I plan to continue the Patreon after the initial 52 pattern releases:

> https://www.patreon.com/knitgrrl

I knit the Milkmaid Mitts, but sample knitters are the unsung heroes of the knit design industry, and don't get nearly enough pay or credit for all their hard work! Here's who helped me bring these designs to life. Many of them are also designers. Look for them on Ravelry!

- Julie Lindsey: Grainne
- Andi Smith: Hildur, Rusla
- Catherine Freedman Myers: Malus Mitts
- Laura Thornton Keevan: Schatzi, Shiso
- Kimber Voutour: Sweet Crocodile
- Caitlin Geronimo: Valencia Marie

At the end of the book you'll also find a list of Patreon patrons. Their project support funded sample knitting, photography, tech editing and all the other expenses required to bring this to life. Thank you, everyone!

Gráinne

Gráinne (pronounced grahn-yeh) is a figure in Irish mythology who eloped with one of her elderly suitor's warriors after forcing him with a geis, a kind of obligatory vow. This Hedgehog Fibres sock yarn will only obligate you to knit with its loveliness, not run away. (Though you could because these socks are super-extra-comfy).

Required Skills

Knitting in the round
Simple increases/decreases
Simple lace from charts or words
Picking up stitches
Kitchener stitch

Size

Women's S (M, L); shown in size M

Intended to be worn with 1 inch / 2.5 cm of negative ease.

Finished Measurements

Circumference: 8.25 (9, 9.75) inches / 21 (23, 24.75) cm

To fit circumference: 9 (10, 11) inches / 23 (25.5, 28) cm

Length: 7.5 (8, 9) inches / 19 (20.25, 23) cm to heel divide

Materials

Hedgehog Fibres Sock (100% superwash merino wool; 437 yds per 100 g skein); color Construct; 1 skein

2 sets of US#1 / 2.25mm 16 inch circular needles needles, or needles needed to get gauge.

Yarn needle

Gauge

32 sts and 38 rounds = 4 inches / 10 cm in pattern stitch

Stitches and Techniques

Gráinne stitch pattern

Rnd 1: P2, k2tog, yo twice, ssk.

Rnd 2: P2, k2, p1, k1.

Rnds 3 & 4: P2, k4.

Repeat Rnds 1-4

Pattern

Using German Twisted, or your preferred stretchy method, cast on 66 (72, 78) sts. Divide sts so that you have 30 (36, 42) sts on the first needle, and 36 (36, 36) sts on the second needle, and, being careful not to twist, join to work in the round.

Rnd 1: *P2, k2, p1, k1; repeat around.

Work repeats of Rnd 1 rib for 1.5 (2, 2.5) inches / 3.75 (5, 6.25) cm.

Work Gráinne chart or stitch pattern words for 6 (6, 6.5) inches / 15.25 (15.25, 16.5) cm, ending after the 4th rnd.

Heel flap prep rnd:

Small: slip next 2 sts to end of previous rnd.

Medium: Slip next st to end of previous rnd.

Large: slip next st to end of previous rnd.

Working with the next 32 (36, 40) sts only:

Row 1: *Sl1, k1; repeat to end of row. Turn.

Row 2: Sl1, p 31 (35, 39). Turn.

Repeat Rows 1 and 2 a total of 17 (19, 21) times.

Heel turn:

Row 1: Sl1, k17 (19, 21), ssk, k1. Turn.

Row 2: Sl1, p5, p2tog, p1. Turn.

Row 3: Sl1, k6, ssk, k1. Turn.

Row 4: Sl1, p7, p2tog, p1. Turn.

Continue in this manner, until all sts have been incorporated.

Gusset:

With RS facing, pick up and knit 17 (19, 21) sts along side of heel flap,

Small: stitch patt over next 30 sts, p2.

Medium: Work in patt as established over next 35 sts, p1.

Large: stitch patt over next 36 sts, p2.

Pick up and knit 17 (19, 21) sts along other side of heel flap, then k to the end of the needle.

This is your new start of rnd.

Rnd 2:

Instep needle: Work patt as established, noting the number of purl sts at the beg and end of the needle may be changed.

Sole needle: K1, ssk, k to last 3 sts of needle, k2tog, k1.

Rnd 3:

Instep needle: Work as established.

Sole needle: Knit.

Repeat Rnds 2 and 3 until you have 66 (72, 78) sts total.

Continue as established, without shaping until foot measures 2 inches less than desired length.

Toe

Small: Slip one st from the end of needle 1 to the beginning of needle 2.

Large: Slip 1 st from end of n2 to beginning of n1.

33 (36, 39) sts on each needle.

Rnd 1: [K1, ssk, k to 3 sts before end

of needle, k2tog, k1] twice.

Rnd 2: Knit.

Repeat Rnds 1 and 2 until 15 (17, 19) sts remain.

Kitchener stitch together toe. Repeat for second sock.

Finishing

Weave in all ends.

Hildur

I posted a preview photo of these on Instagram and my friend (slash- very talented knitter, felter and embroiderer) Harpa Jónsdóttir suggested I call them Hildur (battle), which seemed appropriate given all the other comments referenced them looking like armor somehow!

Required Skills

Knitting in the round

Simple increases/decreases

Simple cables

Picking up stitches

Kitchener stitch

Size

Women's S (M, L); shown in size M

Intended to be worn with 1 inch / 2.5 cm of negative ease.

Finished Measurements

Circumference: 8.25 (9, 9.75) inches / 22.25 (22.75, 24.75) cm

To fit circumference: 9 (10, 11) inches / 24.75 (25.5, 28) cm

Length: 7.5 (8, 9) inches / 19 (20.25, 24.75) cm to heel divide

Materials

Anzula Squishy (80% Merino / 10% Cashmere Goat; 385 yds per 114g skein); color: Lapis; 1 skein

2 sets of US#1 / 2.25mm 16 inch circular needles, or needles needed to get gauge.

Cable needle

Waste yarn for afterthought heel

Yarn needle

Gauge

32 sts and 38 rounds = 4 inches / 10 cm in pattern stitch.

Pattern Notes

When working the 3-st wrap, practice with the wrap to ensure it is snug, but not so tight it distorts the stitches. Too tight a wrap will alter both the gauge and the elasticity of the sock!

Stitches and Techniques

3 st wrap - wyib, slide next 3 sts purlwise to RH needle, bring yarn to front, slide 3 sts back to LH needle,

k1tbl, p1, k1tbl.

1/1 LC - slip next st to cn, hold in front, k1, k1 from cn

1/1 RC - slip next st to cn, hold in back, k1, k1 from cn.

Pattern

Cuff

Using German twisted, or your preferred stretchy method, cast on 64 (72, 80) sts. Divide sts so that you have 32 (32, 40) sts on first needle, and 32 (40, 40) sts on second needle, and, being careful not to twist, join to work in the round.

Work p1, k1tbl rib for 2 (2.25, 2.5) inches / 5 (5.75, 6.25) cm.

Leg

Work repeats of leg chart for 6 (7, 7.5) inches / 15.25 (17.75, 19) cm long, or desired length.

Afterthought heel prep

Medium size only: Knit next 4 sts, and slide to end of second needle. Arrange sts so that you have the next 36 sts on the first needle, and the following 36 sts on the second needle.

All sizes:

Work in pattern as established across first needle. With waste yarn, knit across second needle, then, with working yarn reknit the sts on second needle. Leave the ends of the waste yarn on the outside of your work.

Foot

Work the appropriate foot chart across first needle, and work stockinette across second needle, until, when tried on, sock is 1.5 (2, 2.5) inches / 3.75 (5, 6.25) cm shorter than desired length.

Toe

Rnd 1: [K1, ssk, k to 3 sts before end of needle, k2tog, k1] twice.

Rnd 2: Knit.

Repeat Rnds 1 and 2 until 14 (16, 18) sts remain on each needle.

Use Kitchener stitch to graft toe sts together

Afterthought heel

Working with both needles, and working with two or three stitches at a time, unpick the waste yarn from the heel prep rnd, and slide the upper and lower stitch loops onto two needles. 32 (36, 40) sts on each needle.

Work three rnds in stockinette.

Rnd 4: [K2, ssk, knit to last 4 sts, k2tog, k2] twice.

Rnd 5: Knit

Repeat Rnds 4 and 5 until 12 (14, 16) sts remain

Next rnd: [Ssk, ssk, knit to last 4 sts, k2tog, k2tog] twice.

Finishing

Using Kitchener stitch, graft heel sts together, break yarn, and weave in ends.

Malus Mitts

The domesticated apple, including the Granny Smith cultivar this color brings to mind, is my favorite fruit and a source of constant study as a cider-maker. Every year I bring home endless boxes of hard-to-find cider apples from Rhinebeck and turn them into hard cider for the next year's Sheep and Wool weekend. (Tip: use a farmhouse or saison beer yeast if you make cider, not a wine yeast. It's way more interesting!)

Required Skills

Basic knitting skills

Following pattern from chart

Knitting in the round

Twisted sts

Basic decreases and increases

Size

Women's S (M, L)

Finished Measurements

Hand circumference: 8 (9, 10) inches / 20 (23, 25) cm

Intended to be worn with 0.5 inches / 1.5 cm of negative ease

Materials

Blue Moon Fiber Arts STR Lightweight (100% Merino; 405 yards per 146 gram skein); color: Limestone; 1 skein

2 sets of 16-inch US#1 / 2.25 mm circular needles, or size needed to get gauge

5 removable stitch markers

Stitch holder or waste yarn

Yarn needle

Gauge

30 sts and 34 rounds = 4 inches / 10 cm in stockinette stitch

Stitches and Techniques

1/1 LT - slip next st to cn, hold at front, k1tbl, k1tbl from cn

1/1 LTp - slip next st to cn, hold at front, p1, k1tbl from cn

1/1 RT - slip next st to cn, hold at back, k1tbl, k1tbl from cn

1/1 RTp - slip next st to cn, hold at back, k1tbl, p1 from cn

3 st wrap - [wyib, slip next 3 sts, wyif, slip the 3 sts back to left needle] 3 times, k3

Pattern

Using the German Twisted method, or your favorite stretchy method, cast on 74 (78, 82) sts.

Distribute sts across your needles and join for working in the round.

Ribbing Rnd: *P1, k1tbl; repeat from * around.

Work Ribbing as set for 2 inches / 5 cm.

Next Rnd: K11 (13, 15), pm, work Rnd 1 of chart, pm, k to end of rnd.

Working in pattern as established, work all 14 rnds of chart.

At this point, place a marker or divide the stitches at the halfway point. The first half of the stitches form the back of the hand, the second half the palm.

Decrease Rnd: K2, ssk, work in pattern a set to 4 sts before the halfway mark, k2tog, k2; k2, ssk, k to 4 sts before end, k2tog, k2. 4 sts decreased.

Work 5 rounds even.

Repeat the last 6 rnds 2 more times. 31 (33, 35) sts remain on each side, 62 (66, 70) sts total.

Work even until cuff measures 6 inches / 15 cm, or desired length to base of thumb gusset.

Thumb gusset:

Setup Rnd, Right hand only: Work 31 (33, 35) sts in patt as set, to the halfway mark, k1, pm, kfb, k1, kfb, pm, k to end of round.

Setup Rnd, Left hand only: Work in pattern as set to 4 sts before end of rnd, pm, kfb, k1, kfb, pm, k1. Markers have been place for start and end of thumb gusset, and 2 gusset sts increased.

Rnd 1: Work even in pattern as set.

Rnd 2: Work in pattern as set to first marker, sm, kfb, k to 1 st before marker, kfb, sm, k to end of rnd. 2 gusset sts increased.

Rnd 3: Work even in pattern as set.

Repeat Rnds 2 & 3 5 (6, 7) more times, until you have 15 (17, 19) sts between markers.

Try on your gauntlet. Does it sit comfortably at the join of your thumb? If not, work more rnds without shaping until it does.

Thumb divide

Rnd 1: Work in pattern as set to first marker, remove marker, slip next 15 (17, 19) sts to waste yarn or stitch holder. Cast on 3 sts, remover marker, k to end of rnd. 62 (66, 70)

Hand

Continue even, until when tried on, your gauntlet reaches just below your knuckles.

Work 3 rnds of (p1, k1tbl) ribbing.

Bind off in rib.

Thumb

Return thumb sts back to needles. Rejoin yarn and with RS facing, pick up and knit 3 sts at thumb cast on, and k to end of held sts. 18 (20, 22) sts.

Distribute sts across needles and join for working in the round.

Work in stockinette until when tried on, thumb reaches just below your knuckle.

Work 3 rnds of (p1, k1tbl) ribbing.

Finishing

Bind off in rib. Weave in ends.

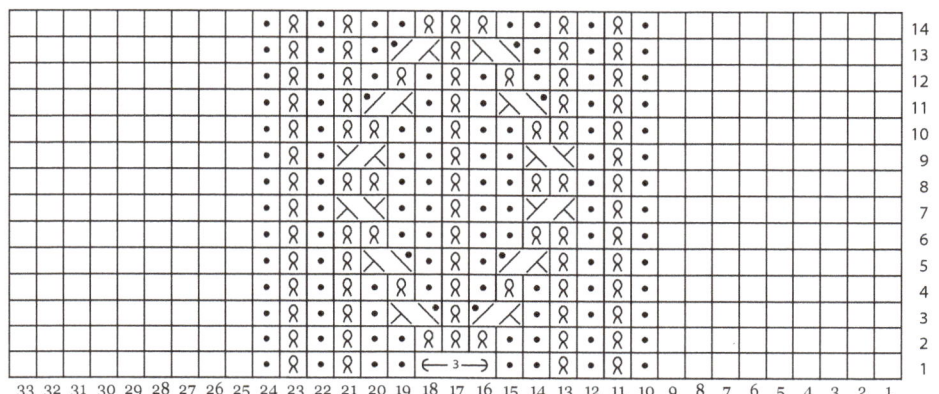

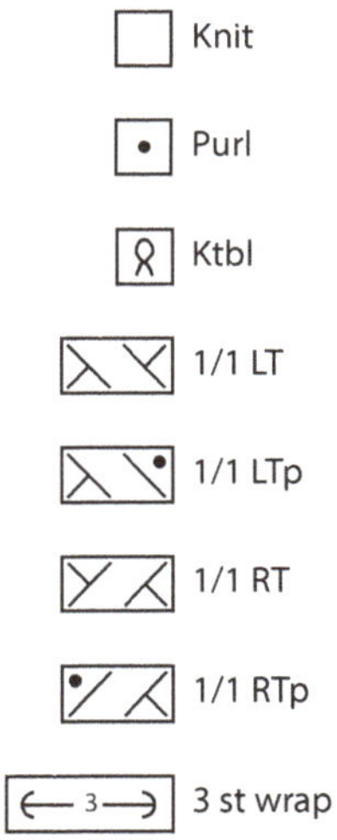

Symbol	Meaning
	Knit
•	Purl
℞	Ktbl
⧅	1/1 LT
⧅	1/1 LTp
⧄	1/1 RT
⧄	1/1 RTp
←3→	3 st wrap

Milkmaid mitts

These are a great quick knit for gifts—and an excellent layering piece on those crazy days when you don't know just what the weather has in store for you. These photos were taken at The Harveyville Project with the original samples, where I teach Felt School every year. I've been dithering on ways to improve these forever and finally decided it was just time to release them as they are!

Required Skills

Basic knitting skills

Simple increases / decreases

Size

S (M, L)

Finished Measurements

Circumference: 6 (8, 10) inches / 15.25 (20.25, 25.5) cm

Height: 8 inches / 20.25 cm

Materials

Malabrigo Worsted (100% Merino; 210 yds / 192m per 100 g skein); color: Purple Magic; 1 skein

US#7 / 4.5 mm needles, configured for flat knitting

Yarn needle

Gauge

20 sts and 32 rows = 4 inches / 10 cm in stockinette stitch

Pattern

Cast on 36 sts, leaving a 16 inch tail, for your non-working yarn.

Row 1(RS): *K1, yo, k2tog; repeat from * to end of row.

Row 2 (WS): Purl.

Rows 3 - 8: *K1, p1; repeat to end of row.

Rows 9, 11, 13, 15: Knit.

Rows 10, 12, 14, 16: Purl.

Rows 17, 19, 21, 23, 25, 27, 29: *K1, p1; repeat from * to end of row.

Rows 18, 20, 22, 24, 26, 28, 30: *P1, k1; repeat from * to end of row.

Rows 31, 33, 35, 37: *P2, k2; repeat from * to end of row.

Rows 32, 34, 36, 38: *K2, p2; repeat from * to end of row.

Row 39: *K1, yo, k2tog; repeat from * to end of row.

Row 40: Purl.

Row 41: *K1, k2tog, yo; repeat from * to end of row.

Row 42: Purl.

Row 43: *K2tog, yo, k1; repeat from * to end of row.

Row 44: Purl.

Row 45: *K1, k2tog, yo; repeat from * to end of row.

Row 46: Purl.

Row 47: *K2tog, yo, k1; repeat from * to end of row.

Row 48: Purl.

Bind off knitwise, leaving a 12 inch tail.

With right sides facing, and side-seams matching, and using the 12 inch tail from the top, whip stitch the seam closed for 2 inches.

Turn the mitt upside down, and using the 16 inch tail from the cast on, whip stitch the seam closed for 4 inches. This will leave a 2 inch gap for your thumb. Weave in all ends.

Finishing

Weave in all ends and block to measurements.

Rusla

This sock is named after a tenth century Viking woman pirate and shield-maiden whose fleet attacked Danish ships and many northern coastlines avenging her brother, whose throne had been stolen. Her sidekick Stikla turned to piracy in order to avoid marriage. Rusla was nicknamed the "Red Maid" and took part in many famous battles. In the end, her enemies grabbed her braids in order to beat her to death with oars. The wrap stitch motif reflects those braids.

Required Skills

Knitting in the round

Working intricate lace from chart or words

Afterthought heel

Kitchener stitch

Size

S (L)

Finished Measurements

Circumference: 8.5 (12) inches / 21.5 (30.5) cm - slightly stretched

Height: 7.5 inches / 19 cm

Materials

Malabrigo Sock (100% Merino; 440 yds / 402 m per 100 g / 3.52 oz); color: Ravelry Red; 1 skein

2 32-inch US#1 / 2.5 mm circular needles, or size needed to obtain gauge

Waste yarn

Large-eyed, blunt needle

Blocking pins

Gauge

36 sts x 40 rnds = 4 inches / 10 cm in stockinette stitch

Pattern Notes

The pattern is written assuming that the knitter is using two circulars, with the first needle (N1) being the "front of leg / front of foot" needle, and the second needle (N2) being the "back of leg/heel / bottom of foot" needle.

If you have problems joining to work in the round without twisting, work the first two rnds back and forth (Row 1: [K6, p1] twice. Row 2: [K1, p6] twice), then join. You will have to stitch up the seam created by those couple of rows, but it eliminates the frustration of a twisted mass in the middle of your work.

Stitches and Techniques

3 st wrap - [wyib, slip next 3 sts to RH needle, wyif, slip 3 sts back to LH needle] three times, k1, yo, k2tog

Rusla stitch pattern - worked over 14 sts

Rnd 1: [K6, p1] twice.

Rnd 2: As Rnd 1.

Rnd 3: Sl1, k2tog, psso, k2, yo, k1, yo, p1, yo, k1, yo, k2, k3tog, p1.

Rnd 4: As Rnd 1.

Rnd 5: Sl1, k2tog, psso, [k1, yo] twice, k1, p1, [k1, yo] twice, k1, k3 tog.

Rnd 6: As Rnd 1.

Rnd 7: Sl1, k2tog, psso, yo, k1, yo, k2, p1, k2, yo, k1, yo, k3tog, pl1.

Rnd 8: As Rnd 1.

Rnd 9: As Rnd 3.

Rnd 10: As Rnd 1.

Rnd 11: As Rnd 5.

Rnd 12: As Rnd 1.

Rnd 13: As Rnd 7.

Rnd 14: As Rnd 1.

Rnd 15: [3 st wrap, p2] twice, 3 st wrap, p1.

Rnd 16: [K1, k1tbl, k1, p2] twice, k1, k1tbl, k1, p1.

Rnds 17 - 24: [K1tbl, p1, k1tbl, p2] twice, [k1tbl, p1] twice.

Rnd 25: As Rnd 15.

Rnd 26: As Rnd 16.

Rnds 27 & 28: [K3, p2] twice, k3.

Rnd 29: As Rnd 15.

Rnd 30: As Rnd 16.

Pattern

Using German Twisted, or your favorite stretchy method, cast on 70 (84) sts, and arrange so that you have 28 (42) sts on N1, and 42 sts on N2.

Join to work in the round, being careful not to twist, and work Rnds 1–30 of Leg Chart once, then Rnds 1–24 once, or work to desired leg length.

Afterthought heel Prep Rnd 1:

N1: Work across sts in patt.

N2: Knit.

Small size only: Slip last 3 sts from end of N2 to beginning of N1, and first 2 sts from beginning of N2 to end of N1. You now have 33 sts on N1, and 37 sts on N2.

Afterthought heel Prep Rnd 2:

N1: P1, k1tbl, p1, work patt as established over next 28 sts, k1tbl, p1.

N2: With waste yarn, knit across all sts, then slide the sts back to beginning of needle. With working yarn, knit across all the sts.

Large size only: Slip last st from end of N2 to beginning of N1. You now have 43 sts on N1, and 41 sts on N2.

Afterthought heel Prep Rnd 2:

N1: P1, work across N1 in pattern as established.

N2: With waste yarn, knit across all sts, then slide the sts back to beginning of needle. With working yarn, knit across all the sts.

Foot

Work N1 as established on last rnd, until foot measures 1.5 (2) inches / 3.75 (5.75) cm shorter than desired length.

Toe

Small size only: Slide the first and last sts on N1 to N2. 35 sts on each needle.

Large size only: Slip the first st from N1 to the end of N2. 42 sts on each needle.

Both sizes

Rnd 1: [K1, ssk, k to 3 sts before end of needle, k2tog, k1] twice. 33 (40) sts on each needle.

Rnd 2: Knit.

Repeat Rnds 1 and 2 until there are 17 (28) sts on each needle, then Rnd 1 only until 11 (12) sts remain on each needle.

Work Kitchener Stitch to close toes.

Heel

Using N1 for top layer of sts, and N2 for bottom layer of sts, and working two or three sts at a time, slowly unpick the waste yarn from the Afterthought Heel Rnd. 37 (41) sts on each needle, 74 (82) sts total.

Rnds 1 & 2: Knit.

Rnd 3: [K1, ssk, k to 3 sts before end of needle, k2tog, k1] twice.

Rnd 4: Knit.

Work repeats of Rnds 3 & 4, until 23 sts remain on each needle, then work Rnd 3 until 18 sts remain on each needle.

Work Kitchener stitch to close the heel.

Finishing

Weave in ends and wet block, taking care to pin the crescents at the top of the socks.

Legend

Symbol	Meaning
☐	Knit
•	Purl
ꕤ (Ktbl symbol)	Ktbl
○	Yo
⋋	K3tog
⋌	Sl1, k2tog, psso
← 3 →	3 st wrap

Chart (Rows 1–30, Stitches 1–14)

Row	14	13	12	11	10	9	8	7	6	5	4	3	2	1
30	•		Ktbl		•	•		Ktbl		•	•		Ktbl	
29	•	←3→	←3→	←3→	•	•	←3→	←3→	←3→	•	•	←3→	←3→	←3→
28	•				•	•				•	•			
27	•				•	•				•	•			
26	•		Ktbl		•	•		Ktbl		•	•		Ktbl	
25	•	←3→	←3→	←3→	•	•	←3→	←3→	←3→	•	•	←3→	←3→	←3→
24	•	Ktbl	•	Ktbl	•	•	Ktbl	•	Ktbl	•	•	Ktbl	•	Ktbl
23	•	Ktbl	•	Ktbl	•	•	Ktbl	•	Ktbl	•	•	Ktbl	•	Ktbl
22	•	Ktbl	•	Ktbl	•	•	Ktbl	•	Ktbl	•	•	Ktbl	•	Ktbl
21	•	Ktbl	•	Ktbl	•	•	Ktbl	•	Ktbl	•	•	Ktbl	•	Ktbl
20	•	Ktbl	•	Ktbl	•	•	Ktbl	•	Ktbl	•	•	Ktbl	•	Ktbl
19	•	Ktbl	•	Ktbl	•	•	Ktbl	•	Ktbl	•	•	Ktbl	•	Ktbl
18	•	Ktbl	•	Ktbl	•	•	Ktbl	•	Ktbl	•	•	Ktbl	•	Ktbl
17	•	Ktbl	•	Ktbl	•	•	Ktbl	•	Ktbl	•	•	Ktbl	•	Ktbl
16	•		Ktbl		•	•		Ktbl		•	•		Ktbl	
15	•	←3→	←3→	←3→	•	•	←3→	←3→	←3→	•	•	←3→	←3→	←3→
14	•							•						
13	•	K3tog	○		○			•			○		○	Sl1,k2tog,psso
12	•							•						
11	•	K3tog		○		○		•		○		○		Sl1,k2tog,psso
10	•							•						
9	•	K3tog			○		○	•	○		○			Sl1,k2tog,psso
8	•							•						
7	•	K3tog	○		○			•			○		○	Sl1,k2tog,psso
6	•							•						
5	•	K3tog		○		○		•		○		○		Sl1,k2tog,psso
4	•							•						
3	•	K3tog			○		○	•	○		○			Sl1,k2tog,psso
2	•							•						
1	•							•						

Schatzi socks

Naming patterns is hard sometimes but the pointy, mountainous "peaks" formed by the pattern immediately reminded me of the mountains we climbed when I studied abroad in Austria. These are named after our favorite German professor's wife there—he constantly called her Schatzi (Darling), it was adorable. Start with that German Twisted cast on and think of Schatzi when you do...

Required Skills

Knitting in the round

Simple increases/decreases

Simple lace (charts or words)

Picking up stitches

Kitchener stitch

Size

Women's S (M, L) ; shown in size M

Intended to be worn with 1 inch / 2.5 cm of negative ease.

Finished Measurements

Circumference: 8.25 (9, 9.75) inches / 21 (22.75, 24.75) cm

To fit circumference: 9 (10, 11) inches / 22.75 (25.5, 28) cm

Length: 7.5 (8, 9) inches / 19 (20.25, 22.75) cm to heel divide

Materials

Malabrigo Yarn Sock (100% wool; 440 yds per 100 g skein); color Turner; 1 skein

2 sets US#1 / 2mm 16-inch circular needles, or size needed to get gauge

Yarn needle

Gauge

32 sts and 38 rounds = 4 inches / 10 cm in pattern stitch

Stitches and Techniques

Schatzi stitch pattern (worked over 8 sts)

Rnd 1: P3, k3, p2.

Rnd 2: P3, k3, p2.

Rnd 3: P2, k2tog, yo, k1, yo, ssk, p1.

Rnd 4: P2, [k1, p1] 3 times.

Rnd 5: P1, k2tog, yo, p1, k1, p1, yo, ssk.

Rnd 6: P1, k1, p5, k1.

Pattern

Using German Twisted, or your preferred stretchy method, cast on 64 (72, 80) sts. Divide sts so that you have 32 (36, 40) sts on the first needle, and 32 (36, 40) sts on the second needle, and, being careful not to twist, join to work in the round.

Rnd 1: *P1, k1; repeat around.

Work repeats of Rnd 1 rib for 1.5 (2, 2.5) inches / 3.75 (5, 6.25) cm.

Work Schatzi chart or stitch pattern words for 6 (6, 6.5) inches / 15.25 (15.25, 16.5) cm, ending after the 6th rnd.

Heel flap

Working with the next 32 (36, 40) sts only:

Row 1: *Sl1, k1; repeat to end of row. Turn.

Row 2: Sl1, p 31 (35, 39). Turn.

Repeat Rows 1 and 2 until heel flap measures approx. 2.5 inches / 6.25 cm.

Heel turn

Row 1: Sl1, k17 (19, 21), ssk, k1. Turn.

Row 2: Sl1, p5, p2tog, p1. Turn.

Row 3: Sl1, k6, ssk, k1. Turn.

Row 4: Sl1, p7, p2tog, p1. Turn.

Continue in this manner, until all sts have been incorporated.

Gusset.

With RS facing, pick up and knit 1 st in each of the slipped sts along side of heel flap, work stitch pattern as established over front of sock, pick up and knit 1 st in each of the slipped sts along other side of heel flap, then knit to the end of the needle.

(New start of rnd.)

Rnd 2: Instep needle: Work patt as established; sole needle: K1, ssk, k to last 3 sts of needle, k2tog, k1.

Rnd 3: Instep needle: Work as established; sole needle: Knit.

Repeat rnds 2 and 3 until you have 64 (72, 80) sts total.

Continue as established, without shaping until foot measures 2 inches / 5 cm less than desired length.

Toe

Rnd 1: [K1, ssk, k to 3 sts before end of needle, k2tog, k1] twice.

Rnd 2: Knit.

Repeat Rnds 1 and 2 until 16 (18, 20) sts remain on each needle.

Use Kitchener stitch to graft toe sts together.

Finishing

Using a tapestry needle, weave in all ends.

Many knitters don't block socks but it really does bloom the yarn and set the stitches, especially with this pair. And it's an excuse to buy some gorgeous sock blockers!

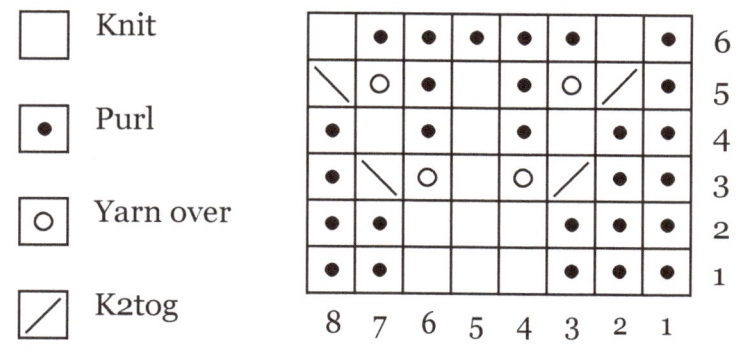

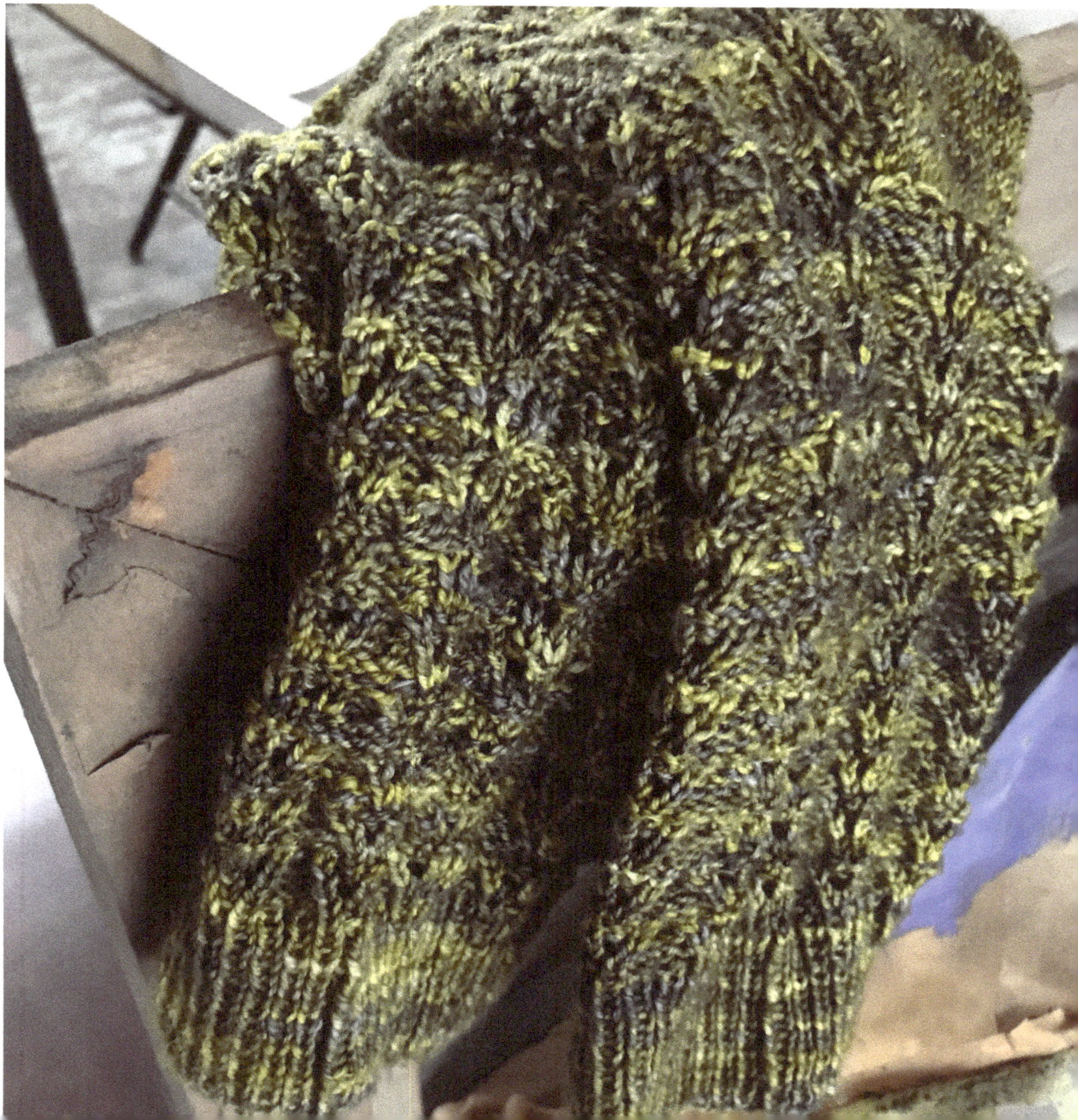

Shiso

Using a k2tog rather than the more conventional ssk in the lace pattern adds texture to this lovely sock. I like how the patterning breaks up the highly variegated yarn but we've added a swatch in plain yellow so you can better see how it looks to the pattern's Ravelry listing.

Required Skills

Knitting in the round

Simple increases/decreases

Simple lace from charts or words

Picking up stitches

Kitchener stitch

Size

Women's S (M, L) ; shown in size M

Intended to be worn with 1 inch / 2.5 cm of negative ease.

Finished Measurements

Circumference: 8.25 (9, 9.75) inches / 21 (22.75, 24.75) cm

To fit circumference: 9 (10, 11) inches / 22.75 (25.5, 28) cm

Length: 7.5 (8, 9) inches / 19 (20.25, 22.75) cm to heel divide

Materials

Spunky Eclectic Tough Sock (100% superwash; 440 yds per 100 g skein); color Angry Hornets; 1 skein

2 sets of US#1 / 2.25mm 16-inch circular needles needles, or size needed to get gauge.

Cable needle

Waste yarn

Yarn needle

Gauge

32 sts and 38 rounds = 4 inches / 10 cm in pattern stitch

Stitches and Techniques

2/2 RC - slip next 2 sts to cn, hold in back, k2, k2 from cn

Shiso stitch pattern (worked over 10 sts)

Rnd 1: P1, 2/2 RC, p1, yo, k2tog, k2.

Rnds 2, 4, 6: [P1, k4] twice.

Rnd 3: P1, k4, p1, k1, yo, k2tog, k1.

Rnd 5: P1, k4, p1, k2, yo, k2tog.

Pattern

Cuff

Using German Twisted, or your preferred stretchy method, cast on 60 (70, 80) sts. Divide sts so that you have 30 (35, 40) sts on the first needle, and 30 (35, 40) sts on the second needle, and, being careful not to twist, join to work in the round.

Rnd 1: *P1, k1; repeat around.

Work repeats of Rnd 1 rib for 1.5 (2, 2.5) inches / 3.75 (5, 6.25) cm.

Leg

Work Shiso chart or stitch pattern words for 6 (6, 6.5) inches / 15.25 (15.25, 16.5) cm, ending after the 6th rnd.

Heel

Afterthought heel prep

Work in pattern as established across first needle. With waste yarn, knit across second needle, then, with working yarn reknit the sts on second needle. Leave the ends of the waste yarn on the outside of your work.

Foot

Continue working pattern as set across first needle, and work stockinette across second needle, until, when tried on, sock is 1.5 (2, 2.5) inches / 3.75 (5, 6.25) cm shorter than desired length.

Toe

Rnd 1: [K1, ssk, k to 3 sts before end of needle, k2tog, k1] twice.

Rnd 2: Knit.

Repeat Rnds 1 and 2 until 15 (17, 19) sts remain on each needle.

Use Kitchener stitch to graft toe sts together

Afterthought heel

Working with both needles, and working with two or three stitches at a time, unpick the waste yarn from the heel prep rnd, and slide the upper and lower stitch loops onto two needles. 30 (35, 40) sts on each needle.

Work three rnds in stockinette.

Rnd 4: [K2, ssk, knit to last 4 sts, k2tog, k2] twice.

Rnd 5: Knit

Repeat Rnds 4 and 5 until 12 (15, 18) sts remain

Next rnd: [Ssk, ssk, knit to last 4 sts, k2tog, k2tog] twice.

Using Kitchener stitch, graft heel sts together, break yarn, and weave in ends.

Finishing

Weave in all ends and block.

Sweet Crocodile

Kimber, my sample knitter for these socks, lives in Florida with a long haired dachshund named Mo who looks exactly like my former dachsie Anezka. This Spunky Eclectic colorway paired with the stitch pattern reminds me of a crocodile, almost like our long-snouted little dog friends. (These days when I hear the word 'crocodile' I think of the St. Vincent song "Krokodil" which has very dachshund-appropriate lyrics: "I need to bite!")

Required Skills

Knitting in the round

Simple increases/decreases

Simple lace from charts or words

Picking up stitches

Kitchener stitch

Size

Women's S (M, L)

Intended to be worn with 1 inch / 2.5 cm of negative ease.

Finished Measurements

Circumference: 8 (9, 10) inches / 20.25 (22.75, 25.5) cm

Materials

Spunky Eclectic Skinny Sock (100% Merino; 340 yds per 100g skein); color: Pulse; 1 skein

US#1 / 2.25 mm needles, or size needed to achieve gauge

Yarn needle

Gauge

32 sts and 38 rounds = 4 inches / 10 cm in pattern stitch

Stitches and Techniques

Sweet Crocodile stitch pattern

Rnd 1: K2tog, [k1, yo] twice, k1, ssk, p1.

Rnd 2 (and all even rnds); K7, p1.

Rnd 3: K2tog, yo, k3, yo, ssk, p1.

Rnd 5: K1, yo, ssk, k1, k2tog, yo, k1, p1.

Rnd 7: K2, yo, sl2, k1, p2sso, yo, k2, p1. Rnd 8: K7, p1.

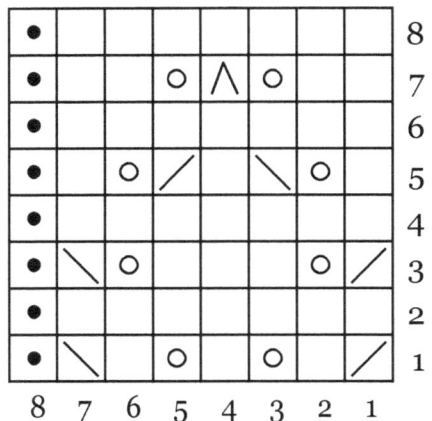

Knit								
• Purl								
o Yo								
/ K2tog								
\ Ssk								
∧ Sl2, k1, p2sso								

Pattern

Cuff

Using German Twisted, or your favorite stretchy method, cast on 64 (72, 80) sts.

Being careful not to twist, join to work in the round.

Rnd 1: *K1, p1, k3, p1, k1, p1; repeat to end of rnd.

Work Rnd 1 until cuff measures 2 (2.25, 2.5) inches / 5 (5.75, 6.25) cm.

Leg

Begin working the Sweet Crocodile stitch pattern from the chart or stitch words above, until your sock measures 6 (6.5, 7) inches / 15.25 (16.5, 17.75) cm from cast on.

Heel Flap

Your heel flap will consist of the first 32 [36, 40] of the 64 [72, 80] stitches.

Row 1: Sl1 k1; repeat from * to end of row.

Row 2: Sl1pw, p to end of row.

Work these two rows a total of 16 times (32 rows) [18 times (36 rows), 20 times (40 rows)].

Heel Turn and Gusset

Row 1: Sl 1 k 18 [20, 22], ssk, k1, turn

Row 2: Sl 1, p7 [7, 7], p2tog, p1, turn

Row 3: Sl 1, knit to one stitch before gap, ssk, k1, turn

Row 4: Sl 1, purl to one stitch before gap, p2tog, p1, turn

Repeat Rows 3 and 4 until all stitches have been worked, but do not slip first stitch on last purl row.

Gusset

Knit across heel stitches and pick up 17 [19, 21] gusset sts along the left side of the heel flap. Work across instep sts in pattern; pick up 17 [19, 21] sts on the other side of the heel flap. The last picked up stitch should be moved to the beginning of the instep sts and incorporated into the instep pattern. The new beginning of round is located between the last heel and first instep stitch. 86 (96, 106) sts

Rnd 1: P1, work across instep sts in pattern as set, k1, ssk, knit to 3 stitches before instep, k2tog k1. (2 gusset sts decreased)

Rnd 2: Work in pattern as set, knitting across gusset sts.

Repeat Rnds 1 & 2 11 (12, 13) times until 64 (72, 80) sts rem.

Work even in pattern as set until foot measures about 2 inches / 5 cm short of desired length.

Toe

Toe set up Rnd: P1 and slip this st to the end of the round. This position is the new start of round.

Decrease round: K1, ssk, k to 3 sts before end of instep, k2tog, k1; k1, ssk, k to 3 sts before end of round, k2tog, k1. 4 sts decreased.

Following round: Knit.

Repeat the last 2 rounds 10 (12, 14) times, until 24 sts remain.

Finishing

Using Kitchener st, graft toe sts together. Break yarn, weave in ends. Block.

Valencia Marie

My friend Daniella's middle name is Marie and she likes to append "Marie" onto anyone's name for humorous purposes, not to mention her own business name (Rebel Marie). If she's scolding me, I'm Shannon Marie (I'm not a Marie. I'm an honorary Marie now). Combine this with her asking me to name a pattern after her, and me already calling these socks Valencia in-studio and well... here we are.

Required Skills

Twisted cable stitches

Working cables from chart or words

Kitchener stitch

Size

S (M, L)

Finished Measurements

Circumference: 8 (10, 12) inches / 20.25 (25.5, 30.5) cm

To be worn with about an inch of negative ease

Materials

Madelinetosh Tosh Sock (100% Superwash Merino Wool; 395 yds / 361 m per 120g / 4.23 oz skein); color: Citrus; 1 skein

US#1 / 2.25 mm needles, configured for circular knitting (2 x 16 inch circulars, 1 x 40 inch circular for magic loop, or 1 set of dpns), or size needed to get gauge

Stitch marker

Cable needle

Waste yarn

Yarn needle

Gauge

32 sts and 44 rnds = 4 inches / 10 cm in pattern stitch.

Stitches and Techniques

1/1 LT - slip 1 st to cn, hold in front, k1tbl, k1tbl from cn

1/1 RT - slip 1 st to cn, hold in back, k1tbl, k1tbl from cn

1/1 LTp - slip 1 st to cn, hold in front, p1, k1tbl from cn

1/1 RTp - slip 1 st to cn, hold in back, k1tbl, p1 from cn

Cuff stitch pattern

Worked over 8 sts

Rnd 1: [P1, k1tbl, k1tbl, p1] twice.

Rnd 2: P1, 1/1LT, p2, 1/1 RT, p1.

Transition Rnds

Rnd 1: [P1, k1tbl, k1tbl, p1] twice.

Rnd 2: P1, 1/1 LTp, p2, 1/1 RTp, p1.

Valencia sock stitch

Rnd 1: P2, 1/1 LT, 1/1RT, p2.

Rnd 2: P2, [ktbl] 4 times, p2.

Rnd 3: As Rnd 2.

Rnd 4: As Rnd 1.

Rnds 5 and 6: As Rnd 2.

Rnd 7: As Rnd 1.

Rnds 8 and 9: As Rnd 2.

Rnd 10: As Rnd 1.

Rnds 11 and 12: As Rnd 2.

Rnd 13: As Rnd 1.

Rnd 14: P1, 1/1 RTp, ktbl twice, 1/1 LTp, p1.

Rnds 15 - 17: [P1, ktbl] twice, [ktbl, p1] twice.

Rnd 18: P1, 1/1 LTp, ktbl twice, 1/1 RTp, p1.

Pattern

Cuff

Using German Twisted, or your favorite stretchy method, cast on 64 (80, 96) sts, and being careful not to twist, join to work in the round, and arrange your sts comfortably across your needle choice. Place a marker to denote the beginning of the rnd.

Working from either the cuff chart, or the cuff stitch pattern, work 2 (2.25, 2.5) inches / 5 (5.75, 6.25) cm.

Transition Rounds

Work the two transition rnds from either the transition chart, or the transition words.

Leg

Following from either the chart or the words, work repeats of the leg pattern until your sock is 6 (6.5, 7) inches / 15.25 (16.5, 17.75) cm long, or your desired length.

Heel Prep

Next rnd: With waste yarn, knit the next 32 (40, 48) sts, slide the sts back to the beginning of the LH needle, and re-knit them with your working yarn. Keeping the ends of the waste yarn to the outside of your work, finish the round working the remaining sts in pattern as established.

Foot

Work the next 32 (40, 48) sts in stockinette, and the following sts in pattern as established.

Continue as set, until foot measures 1.5 (1.75, 2) inches / 3.75 (4.5, 5) cm shorter than final measurement.

Toe

Rnds 1 and 2: Knit.

Rnd 3: [K2, ssk, k24 (32, 40), k2tog, k2] twice.

Rnd 4: Knit.

Rnd 5 [K2, ssk, k22 (30, 38), k2tog, k2] twice.

Rnd 6: Knit.

Continue in pattern as set until you have 32 (40, 48) sts total.

Divide the sts so that you have 16 (20, 24) on each of two needles, and graft together using Kitchener stitch.

Heel

Unraveling a couple of sts at a time from the waste yarn, pick up and knit 32 (40, 48) sts on each of two needles.

Knit 4 rnds.

Work as for the toe.

Finishing

Weave in ends.

Even though I don't normally recommend blocking socks, I do recommend doing so for these. The twisted sts really pop and settle into place with either a wet block or a good steam.

| Ktbl: knit through the back loop

| Purl

1/1 LT: Slip 1 to cn, hold in front, k1, k1tbl from cn

1/1 LTp: Slip 1 to cn, hold in front, p1, k1tbl from cn

1/1 RT: Slip 1 to cn, hold in back, k1tbl, k1 from cn

1/1 RTp: Slip1 to cn, hold in back, k1tbl, p1 from cn

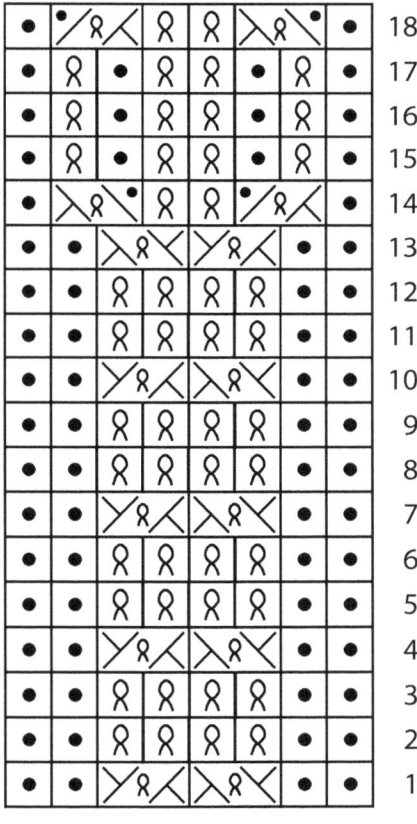

Knitters

Sample knitters are the unsung heroes of the knit design industry and don't get nearly enough pay or credit for all their hard work! Here's who helped me bring these designs to life. Their Ravelry usernames are in parentheses after the pattern they knit—many of my sample knitters are also designers, check out their work!

Julie Lindsey (juri)

Andi Smith (knitbrit)

Catherine Freedman Myers (Mairwen)

Shannon Okey (knitgrrl)

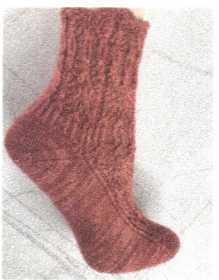
Andi Smith (knitbrit)

Laura Thornton Keevan (LaughingCatFibers)

Laura Thornton Keevan (LaughingCatFibers)

Kimber Voutour (knitkimberknit)

Caitlin Geronimo (spartyjones)

Patron thanks

Almost 300 patrons signed on to support #knitgrrl52 on Patreon from its launch and through the first year. Without their financial support and enthusiasm for the project, I could not possibly have taken on something of this size and complexity. I am incredibly grateful for all of my supporters! This list is current as of 15 May 2018—I plan to continue the Patreon in a modified format, so check out patreon.com/knitgrrl to find out what's going on now! Again, my deepest thanks to all of you!

A. Robin Avila
Afton Koontz
Alicia Harder
Aliza Nevarie
Allison King
Amber F. Lee
Amy Duvendack / BadAmy Knits
Amy Lipkowitz
Amy O'Malley
Amy Shelton
Anna Correll
Anne Smith
Annette Wilhelm
Annie Vanaskie Watters
Antje Gillingham
April Ridgeway
Billy Zayac

Bonnie Callahan
Bonnie Groening
Caitlin Bright
Candice Bailey
Cara Henderson
Carole Chesser
Carolina
Carolyn Blakelock
Carolyn Myers
Catherine Dean
CathiBeaStevenson
Ceri Davies
Charles KNITexan
Chelsea Loo
Cheryl Monroe
Cherylann Schmidt
Chloe Sparkle
Chris Lynch

Christine Jones
Christine Tubbs
Christine Widgren
Conchi Rodes
Crystal Hanson
Dana Kashubeck
Danielle Taylor
Deborah Jackson Weiss
Debra Husby
Debrielle Welch
Dee Minturn
Deenna Dains
Deirdre McNeill
Denise Pratt
Diane Nishri
Dianne Shantz
Dindy Yokel
Donna Hulka

Dorce Campbell
Dragonfly Fibers
Duranee Dodson
Eileen Gruber
Eliza Sheppard
Elizabeth Green
Elizabeth Stromme
Elizabeth Theresa
Ellen Boucher
Erin Mullins
Erin Wolff
Esther Bozak
Faith Love
firstfallen
Fran Bee
Frances McCarthy
Gail E. Maddox
Gaye Houchin-Copeland
Gayle Clow
Glenna Eastwood
Glori Medina
Hanna Hintikka
Hazel Daguiar
Heather Ordover
Heather Risher
Irene Speir
Ivete Tecedor
Jacquilynne Schlesier
Jamie Wang
Jan Arnow
Jan Campagne
Janet Clark
Janice Stenger
Janine Le Cras
Jean Belman-Herrera
Jean Link
Jeanne Tufano
Jeff Pinto
Jenn Ridley
Jenn Wisbeck
Jennifer DeAlmeida
Jennifer Hovis
Jennifer Lindberg
Jennifer Wollesen
Jenny Dicastri
Jenny Schoohs
Jerre Dawson
Jessica Steele
Jessica Stowell
Jillana Holt-Reuter
Joan Grahlfs
Johanna Bowline
Julia Johnson-Roy
Julia Kerbl
Julia Knitterlythings
Julie Aronson
Julie Lindsey
Karen Boykin
Karen Fazioli
Kate Brehe
Kate Graham
Kathryn Beyers
Kathy Beaumont
Katie Hughes
Kelsey Leib
Keri McIntyre
Kim Burkhardt
Kim Fuller
Kimberlee Gillis-Bridges
Kitty Hamersma
Knitty Magazine / Amy Singer
Kristin Hansen
LA Bourgeois
Laura Gilman
Laura, Ben & the 4 Dog Crew
Laurel Luchsinger
Laurie Johnson
Laurie Starr
Lea Vollmer
Lee Bernstein
Leni McCormick
Lesley Robinson
Leslie Behm
Linda Hawkins
Linda Randall
Linda Schiffer
Linda Sutherland
Linda Walker
Lise McKinney
Liz Gipson
Lora Felts
Lorraine Dolsen

Louisa	Nan	Shelley Kinder
Lynn	Natalia Forrest	Shelly Minton
Lynne Wolters	Natalia Uribe Wilson	Stacey Melquist
Magda Stryk Therrien	Niki Curtis	Stacy Person
Margie Smith	Nyriis	Stephanie Mcguckin
Marie Amer-Westmeyer	Pam Daley	Sue Roth
Marie Bryan	Pamela Schultz	Susan Burgerman
Marie Duquette	PariserLandluft	Susan Jones
Marion Gibson	Pat Fisher	Susan Miller
Marion Regeste	Paula Wilson	Susan Wilson
Marsha Auguste	Psuke Bariah	Sylvia McFadden
Marta Poling	Rachel Clark	Sytske Corver
Mary Dagnan Wills	Ray Janikowski	Tammy Moorse
Maureen Foulds	Raymonda Schwartz	Tan A Summers
Meg Helmes	Rebecca Armstrong	Teresa Dannemiller
Melissa Gaul	Relaxing With Yarn	Teresa Emery
Melissa Hellman	Robin Stewart	Terri
Melissa Taylor	Rosemary Moore	Terri Emery
Merlene	Sabrina Pauch	Terri J. Rau
Merry Rubins	Sam B.	Tuulia Salmela
Merryl Rosenthal	Sandra Fleming	Ulla Martin
Meryl Dorey	Sandra Zetterlund	Under MeOxter
Michelle Heckman	Sandy Kolher	Vicki Lynch
Michelle K	Sara Beckwith	Virginia R Jones
Michelle Kennedy	Sarah Devantier	Yael Weiss
Michelle Toich	Shannon Coon	ZhanTao Yang
Monika Stramaglia	Shelley Harper	

www.ingramcontent.com/pod-product-compliance
Lightning Source LLC
Chambersburg PA
CBHW042135160426
43199CB00022B/2920